MAD ABOUT CHELSEA

FACTS, TRIVIA AND QUIZZES FOR DIE-HARD FANS

summersdale

MAD ABOUT CHELSEA

Text by Peter Salmon

An Hachette UK Company
www.hachette.co.uk

Summersdale Publishers
Part of Octopus Publishing Group Limited
Carmelite House
50 Victoria Embankment
LONDON
EC4Y 0DZ
UK

www.summersdale.com

ISBN: 978-1-83799-866-1

To..

From..

INTRODUCTION

They are the London club that can't stop winning. From 2005 onwards (at the time of writing) they have won the Premier League five times, the FA Cup five times, the League Cup three times, the UEFA Europa League twice, the UEFA Super Cup, and greatest of all, the UEFA Champions League – twice!

It all just adds to one of the richest histories in English football – there is no dispute that Chelsea is one of the greatest sides in European history.

With greats like Gianfranco Zola, John Terry, Frank Lampard, Didier Drogba and the King of Stamford Bridge, Peter Osgood, donning the royal blue, there can be no doubt – Chelsea have been a magnet for silverware.

Just as the theme song says, when it comes to football – "Blue is the colour"!

"I still have the shirt signed by the whole Chelsea team from when I was maybe seven or eight."

REECE JAMES

DID YOU KNOW...

Chelsea nearly had a different name. When businessman Gus Mears founded the club on 10 March 1905, at the Rising Sun pub in Fulham, he also considered Kensington FC, Stamford Bridge FC and London FC. But as any fan will tell you – Chelsea is the London football club anyway!

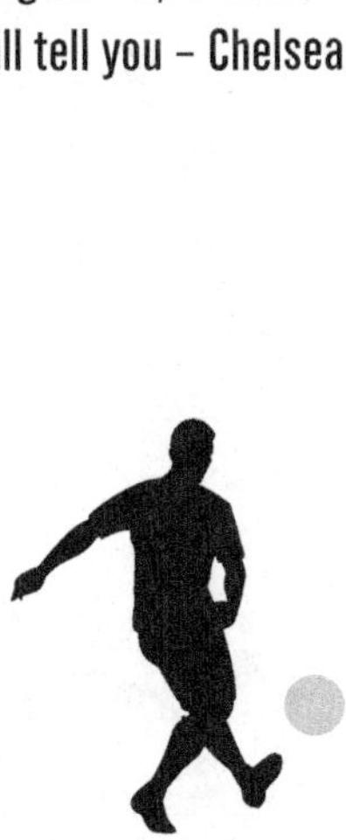

TRIVIA

When Chelsea won the Champions League for the first time, who scored the winning goal in the penalty shootout?

a) Frank Lampard

b) Didier Drogba

c) Juan Mata

> They say the Germans never lose on penalties. They do now.

FRANK LAMPARD

DID YOU KNOW...

When Chelsea won the FA Cup for the first time in 1970, they did so at Old Trafford, home of their bitter rivals Manchester United. The match against Leeds was a replay after a draw at Wembley. Chelsea won 2–1, with the deciding goal scored by Peter Osgood.

TRIVIA

Which player has scored the most goals for Chelsea across all competitions?

a) Frank Lampard

b) Bobby Tambling

c) Gianfranco Zola

Please don't call me arrogant, but I'm European champion and I think I'm a special one.

JOSÉ MOURINHO

DID YOU KNOW...

When José Mourinho took over as manager in 2004, he led Chelsea to their first Premier League victory – and their second the next year! They became only the fifth team since World War Two to go back-to-back in England's top flight. A special one indeed!

TRIVIA

Before there was a Premier League, Chelsea won the First Division in which year?

a) 1935

b) 1955

c) 1975

”

Chelsea is my favourite team. I have always said it, and I have never hidden it.

ROMELU LUKAKU

DID YOU KNOW...

In 1963, bad weather almost cost Chelsea promotion. The freezing conditions that year meant that football was suspended from Boxing Day until February. Division Two leaders Chelsea promptly lost five games in a row – but they managed to win the last two games of the year and went up!

TRIVIA

Roy Bentley was Chelsea's captain when they won the First Division for the first time in 1955 – but who was their top scorer?

a) John McNichol

b) Eric Parsons

c) Roy Bentley

"I spent too little time at Chelsea. I want to have another life so I could spend more time there."

HERNÁN CRESPO

DID YOU KNOW...

Chelsea was one of the first teams to put numbers on their shirts. In their first game of the 1928 season against Swansea Town, they put the numbers to help identify players. Soon after, all the other clubs followed suit. Chelsea won the game 4–0!

?

TRIVIA

Who scored the first goal in Chelsea's history?

a) James Watson

b) James Tait Robertson

c) Jimmy Windridge

My dad was an Arsenal supporter and he used to take me there, but I've always been Chelsea.

ERIC BRISTOW

DID YOU KNOW...

The club was once sold for £1! Back in 1982, Chelsea were struggling financially. Businessman Ken Bates bought the club for a pound. With Bates in charge the club returned to the top flight, often finishing in the top six. Bates sold the club in 2003 – for £140 million!

TRIVIA

Chelsea played their first ever game on 2 September 1905, losing 1-0 to which club?

a) Stockport County

b) Manchester United

c) Lincoln City

”

Chelsea were a sausage, eggs and chips club before the foreign players arrived.

DENNIS WISE

DID YOU KNOW...

Between March 2004 and October 2008, Chelsea did not lose a single League match at home – the longest run of any club in English top-flight history. In total, they were undefeated for 86 games. The next longest is a mere 68 games by Liverpool, and then only 37 by Manchester City.

TRIVIA

Chelsea has never been lower than the second division of English football. But up to 2025, how many times have they been relegated from the top flight?

a) 3

b) 4

c) 6

”

I love Chelsea. I’ve been here seven years now, and I’d love to stay here as long as I can.

ASHLEY COLE

DID YOU KNOW...

Chelsea's longest serving manager is David Calderhead who was at the helm for 26 years, overseeing more than 966 matches. He led the team to the First Division twice in 1912 and 1930, and took them to the FA Cup final in 1915.

TRIVIA

Chelsea has the record for the least goals conceded it in a Premier League season, in 2004-05. How many goals did the opposition score in 38 games?

a) 35

b) 15

c) 25

”

I prefer not to speak. If I speak, I am in big trouble, and I don’t want to be in big trouble.

JOSÉ MOURINHO

DID YOU KNOW...

Chelsea's played in the 1915 FA Cup final, losing to Sheffield United 3-0. The final was nicknamed the Khaki Cup Final as there were so many soldiers in the crowd. It was the last FA Cup final until 1920, two years after the end of the war.

TRIVIA

Who captained Chelsea to five Premier League titles?

a) Dennis Wise

b) Roy Bentley

c) John Terry

"We are lucky to be playing football for a living. For me, this is what I have always wanted to do."

N'GOLO KANTÉ

DID YOU KNOW...

The Chelsea women's football team was established in 1992 and became part of Chelsea FC in 2004. But before that, an unofficial Chelsea Ladies FC had been formed in the 1970s, soon after the Football Association had lifted its 50-year ban on women's football!

TRIVIA

In 1992–93, Andy Townsend was Chelsea's first captain in the Premier League. Who was their first manager?

a) Bobby Campbell

b) Glen Hoddle

c) Ian Porterfield

”

In football, even when you do your best on the pitch, you can win or lose. That is the nature of the game.

GIANFRANCO ZOLA

DID YOU KNOW...

These days Terry Venables is best known as a manager, but as a player he was one of the greatest young talents in Chelsea's history. He made his debut at 17, and when he left at the age of 23 he had already played 234 games and scored 31 goals!

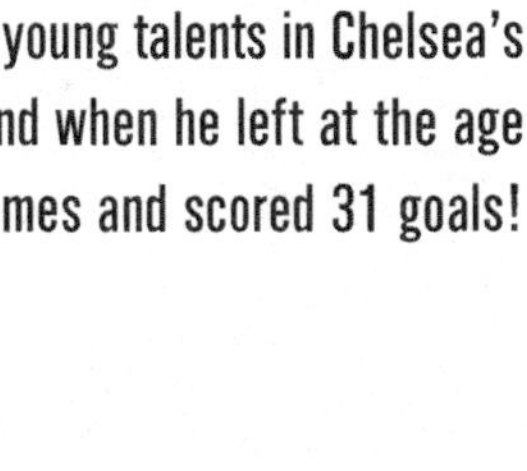

?

TRIVIA

Who scored the winning goal in the 2021 UEFA Champions League final?

a) Timo Werner

b) Mason Mount

c) Kai Havertz

> Football is a collective sport, but goalkeeping is an individual sport.

PETR ČECH

DID YOU KNOW...

Chelsea's first ever goalkeeper William Foulke was famous for his huge size, reaching 24 stone (152 kg/336 lb) at the end of his career in 1908. Legend has it that the football chant "Who ate all the pies?" was first directed at him. He also played first-class cricket!

TRIVIA

Which Chelsea captain had two songs that reached the Top 50 in the UK singles charts, one of them a cover of an Elvis Presley song?

a) Terry Venables

b) William Foulke

c) Willian

99

People will see me at Chelsea the way I am and judge me the way they want to.

EDEN HAZARD

DID YOU KNOW...

Ashley Cole made a controversial switch from Arsenal to Chelsea in 2006 – players don't often transfer to arch-rivals. But Cole would end up playing more games for Chelsea (337) than for Arsenal (156) – but scored one less goal, seven compared to eight. He also played 107 times for England.

TRIVIA

Who captained Chelsea to their last Second Division title in 1988-89

a) Frank Blunstone

b) Joe McLaughlin

c) Graham Roberts

> The best moment was the honour of signing for Chelsea because I was proud to be at such a club.

MICHAEL ESSIEN

DID YOU KNOW...

The American Christian Pulisic played 145 games for Chelsea between 2019 and 2023, but the first player from the US to wear Chelsea colours was Roy Wegerle in 1986. He only played 15 games, but represented the US 41 times. On retirement he became a professional golfer.

TRIVIA

What was the nickname of Ron Harris?

a) Hurricane

b) Chopper

c) The Flea

> **Chelsea are like a beautiful wife who married a richer man after leaving me.**
>
> GIANLUCA VIALLI

DID YOU KNOW...

In 2003, fans voted Gianfranco Zola the greatest player in their history. He played for the Blues 312 times and scored 80 goals for Chelsea between 1996 and 2003, and helped them win five trophies and one community shield. So much was the Italian loved in Britain he was awarded an OBE in 2004.

TRIVIA

José Mourinho led Chelsea to its first Premier League title. Who did he take over from?

a) Ruud Gullit

b) Luiz Felipe Scolari

c) Claudio Ranieri

I love it at Chelsea. All my friends are here, so I'm going to stay for ever.

JOHN TERRY

DID YOU KNOW...

Chelsea's first ever overseas player was the Danish player Nils Middelboe in 1913. Middelboe captained Denmark to the silver medal in the 1912 Olympics. He played 46 games for Chelsea, but still worked in a bank, only playing home games, saying he was "by no means mad about football"!

TRIVIA

How many clean sheets did Petr Čech keep in his 494 games for Chelsea?

a) 140

b) 181

c) 228

”

Acting is my passion, and Chelsea FC is my hobby.

PHIL DANIELS

DID YOU KNOW...

In 1960–61, Jimmy Greaves and Ron Tindall scored an incredible 59 goals between them, a club record. Tindall scored 16 of them, and 67 in his 160-game career. Despite the prolific pair, Chelsea only finished twelfth. Tindall was also a first-class cricketer, scoring two hundreds and taking 150 wickets.

TRIVIA

Defender César Azpilicueta played 349 games for Chelsea between 2012 and 2023. What was his nickname?

a) Bert

b) Max

c) Dave

”

I’m a Chelsea season-ticket holder, and I’ve supported them for 37 years.

SEBASTIAN COE

DID YOU KNOW...

Chelsea has broken the record for the highest transfer fee paid by a British team twice – in 2006 for Andriy Shevchenko, and 2011 for Fernando Torres. Neither striker was successful, Shevchenko scored only 22 times in 77 games, Torres 45 in 172, both well below their normal levels.

TRIVIA

Who was Chelsea manager for the shortest time out of the following?

a) Avram Grant

b) Graham Potter

c) Roberto di Matteo

”

Our number-one opponents are not Liverpool, Arsenal or Manchester United. It is ourselves at Chelsea.

DIDIER DROGBA

DID YOU KNOW...

The last time that Chelsea was relegated was in 1987–88, and amazingly they were sitting second after the first 14 games. They then managed only one win from the next 26, 14 of which were draws. A year later they were back up, and have stayed up since!

TRIVIA

How many goals did centre-back Frank Leboeuf score for Chelsea in the 1997–98 Premier League?

a) 5

b) 12

c) 0

”

I put Chelsea where it should be: at the top.

DIDIER DROGBA

DID YOU KNOW...

In 2009–10, Chelsea became the first team ever to score 100 goals in season, ending with 103. Fourteen different players scored for them, with Didier Drogba scoring 29. They got to the hundred in the final game against Wigan, winning 8–0, with Drogba's header bringing up the ton.

TRIVIA

Who is the oldest player to ever play for Chelsea's first team, aged 41 years and 218 days?

a) Henrique Hilário

b) Mark Schwarzer

c) Ed de Goey

"Never giving in, fighting to the end, that English spirit running right the way through this Champions League for Chelsea."

GARY NEVILLE

DID YOU KNOW...

He has been a regular at every Chelsea game since August 1980 – Stamford the Lion, the club's mascot. It is based on the lion on the Chelsea badge, itself based on the design of the coat of arms of the London Borough of Chelsea, adopted by the club in 1952!

TRIVIA

Who replaced Thomas Tuchel as Chelsea manager in 2022?

a) Graham Potter

b) Frank Lampard

c) Mauricio Pochettino

Losers complain; winners train.

JOSÉ MOURINHO

DID YOU KNOW...

On Boxing Day 1999, against Southampton, Chelsea became the first team to field 11 foreign-born players –manager Gianluca Vialli forced to plug holes in the team after a dose of flu went through the squad. Whatever the reason, it worked – Chelsea won 2–1, Norwegian Tore André Flo scoring twice.

TRIVIA

Which player has won the Chelsea Player of the Year a record four times?

a) Eden Hazard

b) Frank Lampard

c) Juan Mata

I've always been myself. If people find it funny, they find it funny.

COLE PALMER

DID YOU KNOW...

Chelsea won the last FA Cup at the old Wembley before it was re-built – and they won the first at the new Wembley that replaced it. In 2000, Chelsea beat Aston Villa 1–0, and in 2007 they beat Manchester United by the same score, albeit in extra time.

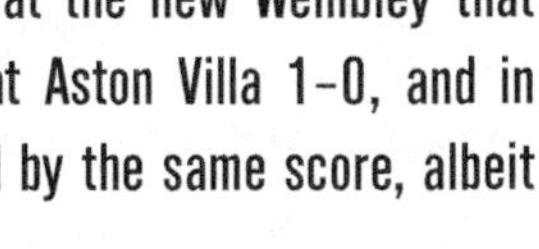

TRIVIA

The Golden Glove is awarded to the Premier League player with the most clean sheets in a season. Petr Čech won it three times. Which other Chelsea goalkeeper has won it?

a) Kepa Arrizabalaga

b) Carlo Cudicini

c) Thibaut Courtois

> I first started going to Chelsea games in the mid nineties when I lived ten minutes' walk from Stamford Bridge.

GEORGE OSBORNE

DID YOU KNOW...

When Chelsea qualified for the first ever European Cup in 1955 by winning the league, they ended up withdrawing from the competition. The head of the FA, Alan Hardaker, argued that domestic competitions should take precedence. Imagine that now – an English team withdrawing from the Champions League!

TRIVIA

Which team has Chelsea not defeated in a Champions League Final?

a) Manchester City

b) Manchester United

c) Bayern Munich

> I joined a club like Chelsea to win titles.
>
> DIEGO COSTA

DID YOU KNOW...

When Kerry Dixon joined Chelsea in 1983, they had been languishing in the Second Division for five years. Dixon scored twice on his debut, 32 for the season, and a hat-trick in the last game that guaranteed they were champions. Dixon played 335 times for Chelsea, scoring193 goals.

TRIVIA

When Graham Potter was sacked as manager in 2023, a Spaniard took over for one match before Frank Lampard was appointed. Who was he?

a) Rafael Benítez

b) Albert Ferrer

c) Bruno Saltor

"

I am not a superstar or an ego. I am just the same as I always was: Someone who plays football.

N'GOLO KANTÉ

DID YOU KNOW...

Claude Makélélé's name in the Bantu language of Lingala means "noises" - and Makélélé made a huge noise for Chelsea, revolutionizing the position of defensive midfielder. The way Makélélé played changed the Premier League to the extent that the position is often called The Makélélé Role, playing in front of the back line.

TRIVIA

In the 2012 Club World Cup final, Chelsea lost 1-0 to their Brazilian opponents. Who were they?

a) São Paulo

b) Corinthians

c) Fluminense

”

José Mourinho doesn’t have a magic wand, where he waves the wand, and everything goes the way you want.

PETR ČECH

DID YOU KNOW...

John Terry is Chelsea's most successful captain, with five Premier League titles, five FA Cups, three League Cups, one Europa League and one Champions League title. He also won many individual honours, including being the first player ever named in the FIFPRO World 11 five times in a row!

TRIVIA

Which defender played 211 games for Chelsea, and didn't score a goal?

a) Gary Cahill

b) William Gallas

c) Allan Craig

John Terry is a great leader. What can I say about him that I haven't said before? He's a great leader.

AVRAM GRANT

DID YOU KNOW...

When Marcel Desailly was named captain of Chelsea in 1998 it was a unique double in the history of the club, as he was also the captain of the French international team. He played a record 116 games for France. At Chelsea, he held the defence together for 222 brilliant games.

TRIVIA

Who won the Premier League Player of the Season award in 2016–17?

a) Nemanja Matić

b) N'Golo Kanté

c) Eden Hazard

”

Watching Ruud Gullit play was like watching an 18-year-old play in a game for 12-year-olds.

GLENN HODDLE

DID YOU KNOW...

Two managers have a 100-per-cent win record for Chelsea, both as caretakers: club legend Ray Wilkins (2009) and Steve Holland (2015). Guus Hiddink won 73 per cent of games as interim manager in 2009, but the best for a permanent manager is 67 per cent – by José Mourinho in his initial spell.

TRIVIA

Who was the first Chelsea manager from outside the United Kingdom?

a) Danny Blachflower

b) Ruud Gullit

c) Gianluca Vialli

”

Why am I the best in the world? Because I am, that's all.

CLAUDE MAKÉLÉLÉ

DID YOU KNOW...

Early in 2000–01, Chelsea's Roberto Di Matteo broke his leg in three places and had to retire, aged just 31, after 175 performances for the club. But it wasn't the end. In 2012, as caretaker manager, he secured both the FA Cup and the club's first Champions League title.

TRIVIA

Michael Ballack played 107 times for Bayern Munich, scoring 44 goals. He played 167 times for Chelsea. How many goals did he score for them?

a) 44

b) 33

c) 26

> Hernán Crespo is my new little lion. And I like lions.

CLAUDIO RANIERI

DID YOU KNOW...

When Reece James became Chelsea captain in 2023, he was the first Chelsea captain to have come all the way through their football academy. He signed for the club at six years old – the future England defender idolized striker Didier Drogba when he was growing up!

TRIVIA

Vinnie Jones, now best known as a Hollywood actor, was also known for collecting 38 yellow cards in his career (as well as 7 red). How many yellows did he get during his 47 games at Chelsea?

a) 11

b) 3

c) 0

”

If Mourinho is Jesus, I am certainly not one of his apostles.

CARLO ANCELOTTI

DID YOU KNOW...

Chelsea's first ever Premier League goal was scored by Mick Harford in his debut for the club, hitting the net in the eighty-fourth minute against Oldham Athletic – who equalized two minutes later, leading to a draw. Harford spent only one season at Chelsea scoring 11 goals in 28 games.

?

TRIVIA

Which member of England's 1966 World Cup winning team went on to manage Chelsea?

a) Geoff Hurst

b) Nobby Stiles

c) Jack Charlton

”

I am not the Special One, I am the Normal One. But my wife says I am the Special One.

AVRAM GRANT

DID YOU KNOW...

The fastest goal ever scored by a Chelsea player was in 1970 – and it took 12 seconds! Keith Weller was in his first and only season for Chelsea when he tore through the Middlesborough defence in the League Cup. Chelsea were 3-0 up after 13 minutes, winning 3-2!

TRIVIA

Who is the youngest player to ever play in Chelsea's first team at 16 years, 4 months and 15 days?

a) Terry Venables

b) Ethan Ampadu

c) Ian Hamilton

I never speak, according to the newspapers. I just storm and blast.

KEN BATES

DID YOU KNOW...

Striker George Hilsdon had a day out for Chelsea on 11 January 1908. He scored six goals against Worksop as Chelsea won 9–1 – still a club record. Hilsdon, nicknamed the Gatling Gun, was the first Chelsea player to score 100 career goals for the club, ending with 108.

TRIVIA

Jimmy Greaves has the record for the most hat-tricks scored by a Chelsea player. How many did he score in his 157 games at the club between 1957 and 1961?

a) 13

b) 15

c) 9

”

Whenever I watch him play, David Luiz looks like he's being controlled by a ten-year-old in the crowd on PlayStation.

GARY NEVILLE

DID YOU KNOW...

The record for most games played for Chelsea in all competitions is held by Ron Harris – he represented the Blues 795 times between 1961 and 1980. He is ahead of goalkeeper Peter Bonetti, with 729 games between 1959 and 1975. John Terry has come closest since, with 717 games.

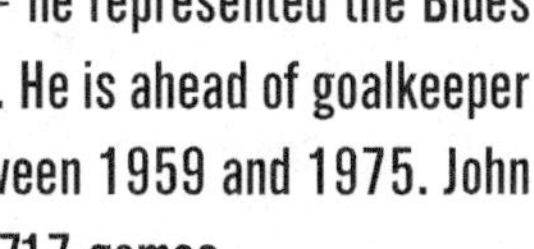

TRIVIA

Who is the oldest player to score a goal for Chelsea?

a) Graham Rix

b) Thiago Silva

c) Glenn Hoddle

"

The ageless Dennis Wise, now in his thirties.

MARTIN TYLER

DID YOU KNOW...

Chelsea has always had celebrity fans, from actors Steve McQueen and Sir Michael Caine to television chef Nigella Lawson. But perhaps the most famous fan is Bill Clinton. The US president used to watch the Blues play back in the 1960s, when he was studying at Oxford!

TRIVIA

Three players have been voted PFA Fans' Player of the Year, Frank Lampard, Eden Hazard and who else?

a) Ashley Cole

b) Cole Palmer

c) Petr Čech

"Helmet on his head, padding on his chin. We like Petr Čech, because he lets no goals in."

FAN CHANT

DID YOU KNOW...

What do you do when your kit organizer forgets to pack your shirts for an away game? Well, you borrow them from the opposition. That's what Chelsea had to do for their game against Coventry on 9 April 1997 – they played wearing Coventry's away strip. Fittingly, they lost 3–1.

TRIVIA

Who was the first Chelsea player to win the Premier League Golden Boot for most goals in a season, scoring three goals in 25 appearances?

a) Didier Drogba

b) Nicolas Anelka

c) Jimmy Floyd Hasselbaink

To go all the way in the Champions League... at this moment, we're the best team in the world.

MASON MOUNT

DID YOU KNOW...

In April 1957, Chelsea became the first club to fly to a domestic fixture, catching a plane to Newcastle for their match on the nineteenth. The new method worked, with Chelsea winning 2–1. Now, of course, most Premier League teams fly to lots of fixtures. Another Chelsea innovation!

FINAL WORD

There is no fan like a Chelsea fan, and no team like the Chelsea team. Glamorous and exciting, Chelsea is always there when the silverware is being handed out, and the trophy cabinet at Stamford Bridge is always full to bursting. What will be their next triumph?

ANSWERS

8 b
11 a
14 b
17 c
20 b
23 a
26 c
29 b
32 c
35 a
38 c
41 a
44 c
47 b
50 c
53 c
56 c
59 b
62 a

65 b

68 a

71 a

74 c

77 b

80 c

83 b

86 c

89 b

92 b

95 c

98 b

101 a

104 c

107 a

110 b

113 b

116 c

Have you enjoyed this book? If so, find us on Facebook at **Summersdale Publishers**, on Twitter/X at **@Summersdale** and on Instagram and TikTok at **@summersdalebooks** and get in touch. We'd love to hear from you!

www.summersdale.com

Image credits

Male footballers © ednal/Shutterstock.com
Female footballers © Eli_Oz/Shutterstock.com
Shirt image © tomambroz/Shutterstock.com

Printed in Great Britain
by Amazon

63032185R00070